GW00993810

Shakesp Kids:

Midsummer Night's Dream

Adapted by CC Beechum
By William Shakespeare

Other books written by CC Beechum

Penelope Barrows #1 The Case of the Blowing Whistle
Penelope Barrows #2 The Case of the Red Sneaker
Penelope Barrows #3 The Case of the Poison Pen Letter

Shakespeare for Kids: Romeo and Juliet
Shakespeare for Kids: Julius Caesar
Shakespeare for Kids: Macbeth
Shakespeare for Kids: Midsummer Night's Dream
(Out in spring 2013.)

Copyright © 2013 by CC Beechum
Recommended for Young Adult Readers

Published by Ebenezer Publishing Co.

This is a work of fiction. Names, characters, places and incidents either are the product of the author's imagination or are used fictitiously, and any resemblance to actual persons, living or dead, events, or locales is entirely coincidental.

Dedication

To every drama club class that ever performed
with me, every performance enriched my life,
as I hope it did yours

Let me begin by saying that all the lines used in the following plays are for the most part verbatim Shakespeare, with a twist here or there. Most of the line is in there, but some were just too long or too confusing for youngsters, so they've been shortened to facilitate use. Some parts are intentionally left out. The main gist of the play is in there, the most important part. Kids love to use these words, it makes them feel important. I would like to believe that Willie would not be upset.

These plays are designed to have a group of children perform them. They take approximately sixty to eighty minutes each play, with a fifteen-minute intermission thrown in. You can however make them shorter or longer if you prefer to. Don't forget about the curtains, stagehands, set designers and a stage manager. These parts are very important in a production of any kind. Some parts can be deleted or added. It's your performance, tailor it to your specific needs. Not everyone wants to be the center of attraction. (Wink,wink.)

I have performed these plays many times, with very diverse groups of children. Each time it was most enjoyable. I have included some stage directions also, please feel free to do whatever you want with them, use them or not. Use your imagination wildly, because the children will definitely use theirs.

And.......action!!!

Midsummer Night's Dream

Cast of Characters

Theseus-Duke of Athens

Bottom

Hippolyta- Queen of the Amazons

Egeus- Father of Hermia

Hermia- Daughter of Egeus, in love with Lysander

Lysander- Loved by Hermia

Helena- In love with Demetrius

Oberon- King of the Fairies

Titiana- Queen of the Fairies

Robin Goodfellow- A Puck (Fairy.)

Fairies 4-6 (Or whatever you choose.)

Attendants- For the King and Queen

Changeling

People at the wedding

Curtains

Narrator

Stage Manager

Midsummer Night's Dream
Enter Narrator

NARRATOR. There are four main strands to Midsummer Night's Dream. One, which forms the basis of the action, shows preparations for the marriage of, Theseus, Duke of Athens, to Hippolyta, Queen of the Amazons, and (In the last act.) its celebration. The second strand is the love story of Lysander and Hermia (Who elope to escape her father's opposition.) and of Demetrius. Shakespeare adds the comic complication of another girl (Helena.) jilted by, but still loving, one of the young men. The third strand is the play for the wedding. I did not include this strand, because the play would be just too long, but I did include the weddings of all the couples at the end of the play. Feel free to add this whole part in if you prefer. The fourth strand Shakespeare depicts a quarrel between Oberon and Titiana, King and Queen of the fairies. Oberon's attendant, Robin Goodfellow, a puck (Pixie.), interferes mischievously in the affairs of the lovers.

(Beginning of play.)

Act One
Scene One
At Hippolyta's castle

Enter Theseus, Hippolyta, and attendants

THESEUS. Now, fair Hippolyta, our nuptial hour draws apace. Four happy days bring in another moon-but O, methinks how slow this old moon wanes!

HIPPOLYTA. Four days will quickly steep themselves in night, four nights will dream away the time. And then the moon, shall behold the night.

THESEUS. Hippolyta, I wooed thee with my sword, and won thy love doing injuries. But I will wed thee in another key-With pomp, with triumph, and with reveling.

Enter Egeus, Hermia, Lysander, and Demetrius

EGEUS. Happy be Theseus, our renowned Duke!

THESEUS. Thanks, good Egeus. What's the news with thee?

EGEUS. Full of vexation come I, with the complaint against my daughter, Hermia. Stand forth Demetrius. This hath my consent to marry her. Stand forth Lysander. And, this man hath bewitched my child into loving him. I beg the ancient privilege of Athens. As she is mine, to dispose of her to this gentleman, (Pointing to Demetrius.) or to her death, according to our law.

THESEUS. What say you Hermia? Demetrius is a worthy gentleman.

HERMIA. So is Lysander!

THESEUS. In himself he is. But in your father's voice, the other must be held the worthier.

HERMIA. I would my father looked but with my eyes.

THESEUS. Rather your eyes must with his judgement look.

HERMIA. I do entreat your grace to pardon me. I know not by what power I am made bold. But I beseech your grace that I may know. The worst that may befall me in this case. If I refuse to wed Demetrius.

THESEUS. Either to die the death or marry who I say. For ever the society of men. Whether, if you yield not to your father's choice, you can endure the life of a nun.

HERMIA. So will I grow, so live, so die, my lord. (Kneel at his feet.)

THESEUS. (Take her hand to stand up.) Take time to pause, and by the next new moon- the sealing day, decide. For disobedience to thy father's will, upon that day prepare to die. Or else to wed Demetrius.

DEMETRIUS. Relent, sweet Hermia, and Lysander yield.

LYSANDER. You have your father's love, Demetrius. Let me have Hermia's.

EGEUS. Scornful Lysander! True, ha hath my love. And what is mine I do estate unto Demetrius.

LYSANDER. I am my lord, as well derived as he. My love is more than his. I am beloved of beauteous Hermia. Why should not I then prosecute my right?

THESEUS. I must confess that I have heard so much. And with Demetrius thought to have spoke thereof. But Demetrius come, and, come Egeus. You shall go with me, I have some private schooling for you both. Come Hippolyta, go along, go along, I must employ you in some business.

EGEUS. With duty and desire we follow you.

Exit all except Lysander and Hermia

LYSANDER. How now, my love? Why is your cheek so pale? How chance the roses there do fade so fast?

HERMIA. O spite! Too old to be engaged so young.

LYSANDER. Ay me, for aught that I could ever read the course of true love never did run smooth.

HERMIA. Oh cross! To choose by another's eyes! If then true love have never been crossed. But, it is customary cross, to teach patience.

LYSANDER. Therefore hear me Hermia. I have a widow aunt, a dowager of great revenue, and she hath no child, and she respects me as her only son. From Athens is her house, remote. There, gentle Hermia may I marry thee, and to that place Athenian law cannot pursue us. Steal forth thy father's house tomorrow night, and in the wood, there I will stay for thee.

HERMIA. My good Lysander, I swear to thee by Cupid's strongest bow, in that same place thou hast appointed me tomorrow truly will I meet with thee.

LYSANDER. Keep promise, Love. Look, here comes Helena.

Enter Helena

HERMIA. God speed, fair Helena. Wither away?

HELENA. Call you me fair? That 'fair' again unsay. Demetrius loves your fair- O happy fair!! O, teach me how you look, and with what art you sway the motion of Demetrius' heart.

HERMIA. I frown upon him, yet he loves me still.

HELENA. O that your frowns would teach my smiles such skill!

HERMIA. I give him curses, yet he gives me love.

HELENA. O that my prayers could such affection move!

HERMIA. The more I hate, the more he follows me.

HELENA. The more I love, the more he hateth me.

HERMIA. His folly, Helen, is no fault of mine.

HELENA. None but your beauty; would that fault were mine!

HERMIA. Take comfort. He no more shall see my face. Lysander and myself will fly this place.

LYSANDER. Helen, to you our minds we will unfold. Tomorrow night, when Phoebe doth behold, a time that lover's sleights doth still conceal- Through Athens gates have we devised to steal.

HERMIA. And in the wood where often you and I lie. There my Lysander and myself shall meet. And thence from Athens turn away our eyes. Farewell, sweet playfellow. Pray thou for us, and good luck thee thy Demetrius. Keep word, Lysander. From lovers food till morrow deep midnight.

LYSANDER. I will, my Hermia. Helena adieu.

Exit Hermia and Lysander

HELENA. (Alone.) How happy some o'er other some can be! Through Athens I am thought as fair as she. But what of that?

Demetrius thinks not so. Love can transpose to form and dignity. Love looks not with the eyes, but with the mind, and therefore is winged cupid painted blind.

Act One
Scene Two
Fairy Forest, night

Enter Robin and Fairy

ROBIN. How now, spirit, whither wander you?

FAIRY. Over hill, over dale. Thorough bush, thorough brier, over park, over pale, thorough fire. I do wander everywhere. I serve the Fairy Queen. I must seek some dewdrops here, and hang a pearl in every cowslips ear. Farewell, thou lob of spirits. I'll be gone our Queen and all her elves come here anon.

ROBIN. The king doth keep his revels here tonight. Take heed the Queen come not within his sight. For Oberon is passing fell and wroth. Because that she, as her attendant, hath a lovely boy stol'n from an Indian king. She never had so sweet a changeling: And jealous Oberon would have the child. But she perforce withholds the loved boy, Crown him with flowers, and makes him all her joy.

FAIRY. Either I mistake your shape, or else you are that shrewd and knavish sprite called Robin Goodfellow. Are not you he? That frights the maidens of the villag'ry. Mislead night wanderers, laughing at their harm? Those that hobgoblin call you, and sweet puck, you do their work, and shall have good luck. Are not you he?

ROBIN. Thou speak'st aright. I am that merry wanderer of the night A merry hour was never wasted. But make room, fairy. Here comes Oberon.

Enter Oberon and Titiana (With fairies.)

FAIRY. And here my mistress. Would that he were gone.

OBERON. I'll met by moonlight, proud Titiana.

TITIANA. What, jealous Oberon? Fairies skip hence. (Fairies skip.)

OBERON. Tarry, rash wanton. Am I not thy Lord?

TITIANA. Then I must be thy Lady. But I know when thou hast stol'n away from fairyland. Why art thou here?

OBERON. Why indeed? Do you amend it then? It lies in you. Why should Titiana cross Oberon. I do but beg a little changeling boy to be my henchman.

TITIANA. Set your heart at rest. The fairyland buys not the child of me. His mother was a vot'ress of my order. But she, being mortal, of that boy did die. And for her sake do I rear up the boy. And for her sake I will not part with him.

OBERON. How long within this wood intend you stay?

TITIANA. Perchance till after Theseus' wedding day. If not, shun me, and I will spare your haunts.

OBERON. Give me that boy and I will go with thee.

TITIANA. Not for thy kingdom. Fairies away. (Fairies flutter away.) We shall chide downright if I longer stay.

Exit Titiana

OBERON. Well go thy way. Thou shalt not from this grove. My gentle Puck, come hither. Thou rememb'rest once I sat upon a dolphins back? And certain stars madly from their spears to hear the sea-maids music?

ROBIN. (Puck.) Yes my Lord.

OBERON. That very time I saw, but thou couldst not see young cupid's fiery shaft. Yet marked I where the bolt of Cupid fell. It fell upon a little western flower. Before, milk-white; now, purple with love's wound. And maidens call it love-in-idleness. Fetch me that flower. The herb I showed thee once. The juice of it on sleeping eyelids laid. Will make man or woman madly dote upon the next living creature that it sees. Fetch me this herb, and be thou here again.

ROBIN. I'll put a rope round the earth in forty.

Exit Robin, alone

OBERON. (Alone.) Having once this I'll Titiana when she is asleep, and drop this liquid in her eyes. The next thing she looks upon, be it lion, bear, wolf, or bull, she shall fall madly in love there with. And ere I take this charm from off her sight, I'll make her render up her page to me. But who comes here? I am invisible. And I will overhear this conference.

Enter Demetrius and Helena
Oberon overhears conversation.

DEMETRIUS. I love thee not, therefore pursue
me not. Where is Lysander, and fair Hermia?
The one I'll slay, the other slayeth me. Thou
told'st me they were stol'n unto this wood.
Because I cannot meet Hermia hence, get thee
gone, and follow me no more.

HELENA. You draw me, you hard-hearted
adamant. But yet you draw not iron: for my
heart is true steel. Leave you your power to
draw, and I shall have no power to follow.

DEMETRIUS. Do I entice you? Do I speak you
fair? Or rather do I not in plainest truth tell you
I do not nor I cannot love you?

HELENA. And even for that do I love you
more. I am your spaniel, and Demetrius the
more you beat me I will fawn on you.

upon her love; and thou meet me ere the first cock crow.

ROBIN. Fear not, my lord, your servant shall do so.

Exit both

Act Two
Scene Two
Fairy Forest, night

Enter Titiana, Queen of Fairies and her train of fairies

TITIANA. Come, now a roundel and a fairy song. Sing me now asleep. Then to your offices, and let me rest. (She lies down.)

Fairies sing.

CHORUS. Lulla, lulla, lullaby. Lulla, lulla, lullaby. Never harm, nor spell nor charm. Come our lovely lady nigh. So good night, with lullaby.

Titiana sleeps, fairies sleep as well.

Enter Oberon
He drops the juice on Titiana's eyelids.

OBERON. What thou sees when thou dost wake. Do it for thy true love take. In thy eye that shall appear. When thou wak'st, it is thy dear. Wake when some vile thing is near.

Curtain closes.

Act Three
Scene One
Fairy Forest, day

Enter Lysander and Hermia

LYSANDER. Faie love, you faint with wand'ring in the wood. I have forgot our way. We'll rest us, Hermia, if you think it good. And tarry for the comfort of the day.

HERMIA. Be it so, Lysander. Find you out a bed. For I upon this bank will rest my head. (She lies down.)

LYSANDER. Amen, amen, to that fair prayer say I. Here is my bed, sleep give thee all his rest. (He lies down, they fall asleep.)

HERMIA. With half that wish the wisher's eyes be pressed.

Enter Robin

ROBIN. Through the forest have I gone, but Athenian found I none. Night and silence. Who is here? Weeds of Athens he doth wear. This is he my master said. Churl, upon thy eyes I throw. All the power this charm doth owe. (He drops the juice on Lysander's eyelids.) When thou wak'st, let love forbid. Sleep his seat on thy lid. So, awake when I am gone. For I must now to Oberon.

Enter Demetrius and Helena running

HELENA. Stay, though thou kill me sweet Demetrius.

DEMETRIUS. I charge thee hence, and do not haunt me thus.

HELENA. O, wilt thou darkling leave me? Do not so.

DEMETRIUS. Stay, on thy peril. I alone will go.

HELENA. O, I am out of breath in this fond chase. Happy is Hermia, wheresoe'er she lies. For she hath blessed and attractive eyes. No, no; I am ugly as a bear. For beasts that meet me run away for fear. But who is here? Lysander, on the ground? Dead, or asleep? I see no blood. No wound. Lysander, if you live, good sir, awake.

LYSANDER. (Awaking.) Where is Demetrius? O, how fit a word. Is that vile name to perish on my sword?

HELENA. Do not say so, Lysander; say not so. What thou he love your Hermia? Lord, what thou? Yet Hermia still loves you; then be content.

LYSANDER. Content with Hermia? No, I do repent. The tedious minutes I have spent! Not Hermia but Helena I love. And reason says you are the worthier maid. And leads me to your eyes, where I o'erlook. Love's stories written in love's richest book.

HELENA. Wherefore was I to this keen mockery born? When at your hands did I deserve this scorn? Is't not enough, is't not enough, young man. That I did never-no nor ever can. Deserve a sweet look from Demetrius' eye. But fare you well. Perforce I must confess I thought you lord of more true gentleness.

LYSANDER. She sees Hermia. Hermia, sleep thou there. And never mayst thou come Lysander near. Of all be hated, but most of me. And all my powers, address your love and might to honour Helen, and to be her knight.

HERMIA. (Awaking.) Help me, Lysander, help me! Do thy best to pluck this crawling serpent from me. Ay me, for pity. What a dream was here? Lysander, look how I do quake with fear, Lysander what removed? Lysander, lord- What, out of hearing gone? No sound, no word? Alack, where are you ? Speak if you hear. Speak, of all loves. I swoon almost with fear. No? Then I will think you are not nigh. Either death or you I'll find immediately.

Act Three
Scene Two
Fairy Forest, day

TITIANA. (Awaking.) What angel wakes me from my flow'ry bed?

BOTTOM. The finch, the sparrow and the lark. Whose note full many a man doth mark. And dares not answer nay? (Singing.) I am on my way to a masked ball. Lalalalala (He has a donkey's head mask on.)

You must convey somehow that he is going to a masquerade ball.

TITIANA. I pray thee, gentle mortal, sing again. On the first view to say, to swear, I love thee.

BOTTOM. Methinks, mistress, you should have little reason for that. And yet, to say the truth, reason and love keep little company together nowadays.

TITIANA. Thou art as wise as thou art beautiful.

BOTTOM. Not so, neither; but if I had wit enough to get out of this wood, I have enough to serve mine own turn.

TITIANA. Out of this wood do not desire to go. Thou shalt remain here, whether thou wilt or no. And I do love thee. Therefore go with me.

I'll give thee fairies to attend on thee, and they shall fetch thee jewels from the deep, and sing while thou on pressed flowers dost sleep.

Enter four fairies: Peaseblossom, Cob Webb, Mote, and Mustardseed

PEASEBLOSSOM. Ready.

COB WEBB. And I.

MOTE. And I.

MUSTARDSEED. And I.

ALL FOUR FAIRIES. Where shall we go?

TITIANA. Be kind and courteous to this gentleman. Feed him with apricots and dew-berries.

MUSTARDSEED. And pluck the wings from painted butterflies to fan moonbeams from his sleeping eyes.

PEASEBLOSSOM. Hail mortal. (To Bottom.)

COB WEBB. Hail.

MOTE. Hail.

MUSTARDSEED. Hail.

BOTTOM. I cry your worship's mercy, heartily - I beseech your worship's name.

COBWEBB. Cobwebb.

TITIANA. (To fairies.) Come, wait upon him, lead him to my bower. Tie up my love's tongue: bring him silently. (Fetch him food, feed him, wait on him.)

Exit all

Act Three
Scene Three
Fairy Forest, day

Enter Oberon, King of the fairies

OBERON. I wonder if Titiana be awaked, then what it was that next came in her eye, which she must dote on in extremity.

Enter Robin Goodfellow

OBERON. Here comes my messenger. How now mad spirit?

ROBIN. My mistress with a monster is in love. While she was in her dull and sleeping hour, why she spied and walked straightway in love with a …. Donkey!

OBERON. This falls out better than I could devise; but hast thou yet latched the Athenian's eyes with the love juice? As I did bid thee do?

ROBIN. I took him sleeping; that is finished too, and the Athenian woman by his side, that when he waked of force she must be eyed.

Enter Demetrius and Hermia

OBERON. Stand close. This is the same Athenian.

ROBIN. This is the woman, but not this the man!

DEMETRIUS. O, why rebuke you him that loves you so? Lay breath so bitter on your bitter foe.

HERMIA. What's this to my Lysander? Where is he? Ah, good Demetrius, wilt thou give him to me?

DEMETRIUS. I had rather give his carcass to my hounds.

HERMIA. Out, dog; out, cur. Thou driv'st past the bounds of maiden's patience. Hast thou slain him then? O, once tell true; tell true, even for my sake. And hast thou killed him sleeping?

DEMETRIUS. You spend your passion on a misprised mood. I am not guilty of Lysander's blood. Nor is he dead, for aught that I can tell.

HERMIA. I pray thee, tell me then that he is well.

DEMETRIUS. And if I could, what should I get therefore?

HERMIA. A privilege never to see me more. And from thy hated presence part I so. See me no more, whether he be dead or no.

DEMETRIUS. There is no following her in this fierce vein. For debt that bankrupt sleep doth sorrow owe. Which now in some slight measure it will pay, if for his tender here I make some stay. (He lies down to sleep.)

OBERON. (To Robin.) What hast thou done? Thou hast mistaken quite. And laid the love juice on some true love's sight. Some true love turned, and not a false turned true? About the wood go swifter than the wind. And Helena of

Athens look thou find. By some illusion see thou bring her here I'll charm his eyes against she do appear.

ROBIN. I go, I go-look how I go, swifter than arrow from the Tarter's bow. (He runs off.)

OBERON. (Casting a spell over Demetrius.) Flower of this purple dye, hit Cupid's archery, sink in apple of his eye. (He drops the juice on Demetrius' eyelids.) When his love he doth espy, let her shine as gloriously as Venus of the sky. When thou wak'st, if she be by, beg of her for remedy.

Act Four
Scene One
Fairy Forest, night

ROBIN. Captain of our fairy band, Helena is here at hand, (Pointing off stage.) And the youth mistook by me, pleading for a lover's fee. Lord, what fools theses mortals be.

OBERON. Stand aside. The noise they make, will cause Demetrius to awake.

ROBIN. Then will two at once woo one. That must needs sport, and those things do best please me that befall. (They stand apart.)

Enter Helena, Lysander following her

LYSANDER. Why should you think that I should woo in scorn? How can these things in me seem to scorn you, Bearing the badge of faith to prove them true.

HELENA. You do advance your cunning more and more. When truth kills truth- O devilish holy fray! These vows are Hermia's. Will you give her o'er?

LYSANDER. I had no judgement when to her I swore. Demetrius loves her, and he loves you not.

DEMETRIUS. (Awaking.) O Helen, goddess, perfect, divine! O, let me kiss thy hand! The princess of pure white.

HELENA. O spite! I see you are all bent to set against me for your merriment!

LYSANDER. You are unkind, Demetrius. Be not so. For you love Hermia; this you know. And here with all good will, with all my heart, In Hermia's love I yield you up my part.

HELENA. Never did mockers waste more idle breath.

DEMETRIUS. Lysander, keep thy Hermia. I will none. If e'er I loved her, all that love is gone. My heart to her but as guestwise sojourned and now to Helen is it returned, there to remain.

LYSANDER. Helen, it is not so.

DEMETRIUS. Look where thy love comes; yonder is thy dear.

HERMIA. Thou art not by mine eye, Lysander found, but why unkindly didst thou leave me so?

LYSANDER. Why should he stay whom love doth press to go? The hate I bare thee made me leave so?

HERMIA. You speak not as you think. It can not be!

HELENA. (Whisper to the side, to audience.) Now I perceive they have conjoined all three? To fashion this false sport in spite of me.

HERMIA. I am amazed at your passionate words. I scorn you not. It seems you scorn me.

HELENA. Have you not set Lysander, as in scorn to follow me? And made your other love Demetrius spurn me with his foot?

HERMIA. I understand not what you mean by this?

HELENA. Ay do! Make mouths upon me when I turn my back. Death or absence soon shall remedy.

LYSANDER. Stay gentle Helena, hear my excuse. My love, my life, my soul, fair Helena!

HELENA. O excellent!

LYSANDER. Helen, I love thee; by my life I do.

DEMETRIUS. (To Helena.) I say I love thee more than he can do.

Hermia cries and paces.

LYSANDER. Prove it! (To Demetrius.)

DEMETRIUS. Quick come!

HERMIA. Lysander where to tends all this? (She takes him by the arm.)

LYSANDER. Away you!

DEMETRIUS. No, no sir yield. You are tame man, go!

LYSANDER. (To Hermia.) Hang off. Let loose. Or I will shake thee from me like a serpent.

HERMIA. Why have you grown so rude? What change is this sweet love?

LYSANDER. Thy love? Out! O hated potion, hence. (He realizes a spell was cast on him.)

Curtain

Act Four
Scene Two
Forest

Enter Oberon and Robin, attendants

OBERON. This is thy negligence. (To Robin.)

ROBIN. Believe me king of shadows, I mistook. Did you not tell me I should know the man by his Athenian garments? (Points to Lysander.)

OBERON. Thou seest these lovers seek a place to fight. We must right this wrong upon these men. Crush this herb into Lysander's eyes to take all error away. When they next wake shall seem a dream to them. Back to Athens shall the lovers hence. And while in this do thee employ I'll go to my queen and beg back the Indian boy. And then I will her charmed eye release from the monsters view and all shall be in peace.

ROBIN. My fairy lord, this must be done with haste. (He starts the spell.) Up and down, up and down. I will lead them up and down. Here comes one now.

ATTENDANT. Goblin, lead them up and down.

ATTENDANT. Here comes one.

Enter Lysander

LYSANDER. Where art thou Demetrius? Speak thee now!

ROBIN. (Pretending to be Demetrius, hiding.) Here, villain, drawn and ready. Where art thou?

LYSANDER. (Looking confused.) I will be with thee straight. (Drawing his sword.)

ROBIN. (Hiding.) Follow me then.

Lysander follows voice.

DEMETRIUS. Lysander speak again. Thou run away. Thy coward. Speak. In some bush?

ROBIN. (Hiding, shifting position.) Thou coward, telling the bushes that thou lookst' for wars? Draw a sword on thee.

DEMETRIUS. Yea, art thou there?

ROBIN. Follow my voice. And wilt not come.

LYSANDER. What is thou there? When I come where he calls, then he is gone. The villain is much lighter heeled than I. I followed fast but did he fly. Here will rest me. (He lies down.)

DEMETRIUS. Where art thou now? Thou runnest before me, shifting every place. Faintncss overpower me. (He lies down.)

Enter Helena

HELENA. Oh weary night. So that I may back to Athens by daylight. (She yawns and lies down.)

ROBIN. (Coming out of the forest.) Yet but three? Come one more. Two of both kinds makes up four.

Enter Hermia

ROBIN. Here she comes curst and sad. Cupid is a knavish lad.

HERMIA. Never so weary, never so in, Woe!
I can no further crawl, no further go. (She lies
down.)

ROBIN. On the ground sleep sound. I'll apply
to your eye, gentle lover remedy. (He drops
juice on Lysander's eyelids.) When thou wak'st
thou tak'st true delight in the sight of thy former
lady's eye. Jack shall Jill, naught shall go ill.

Act Four
Scene Three
Fairy Forest, day

Enter Titiana, Bottom, (With a donkey's head
on.) fairies

TITIANA. (To Bottom.) Come, sit thee down
upon thy flow'ry bed. And kiss thy large ears.
(Kisses his ears.) Wilt thou hear some music
my sweet love?

BOTTOM. I have a good ear in music. Let's
have some.

Music plays, and fairies dance and sing.

TITIANA. Or sweet love desir'st to eat? Some peanuts per chance?

BOTTOM. Methinks I would rather a handful of two dried peas.

TITIANA. Sleep thou now, fairies be gone. (She waves her hand.) They fall asleep.

Enter Robin and Oberon (Meeting.)

OBERON. Welcome. Good Robin. See'st thou sweet sight? I do begin to pity. I will undo this hateful vex of her eyes. (He drops the juice in her eyelids.) Be as thou wast won't to be. See as thou wast won't to see. Now wake my Titiana, wake you, my sweet queen.

TITIANA. (Yawns.) My Oberon, what visions have I seen. Methinks I was in love with a fool!

OBERON. There lies your love.

TITIANA. How came these things to pass? O, how mine eyes do hate this donkey now.

OBERON. Silence awhile. Robin do take off his head.

Robin takes donkey head off Bottom.

OBERON. Sound music. (Music plays.) Come my queen, take hands with me.
(Oberon and Titiana dance.)

ROBIN. Hark fairy king, I do hear the morning lark sing.

TITIANA. Come, my lord and in our flight tell me how it came this night to find these mortals sleeping on the ground. (Pointing to mortals.)

Enter Theseus, Egeus, Hippolyta and train
(Horns sound.)

THESEUS. Go, go one of you, go find them!

EGEUS. My lord, methinks this is my daughter here asleep. And this is Lysander, this Demetrius, and this Helena.

THESEUS. No doubt they rose up early. But speak Egeus, is this not the day that Hermia should give answer of her choice?

EGEUS. It is, my lord.

THESEUS. Go with the huntsman wake them with their horns. (Horns blow.)

The lovers all stand up.

THESEUS. Good morrow friends. Saint Valentine is past.

LYSANDER. Pardon my lord. (They all kneel.)

THESEUS. I pray you all stand up. (Lovers stand.) (To Demetrius and Lysander.) I know you two are rival enemies. To sleep by hate and fear no pain?

LYSANDER. My lord, I shall reply amazedly. I cannot truly say how I came here. I came with Hermia hither, to be gone from Athens where we might marry.

EGEUS. (To Theseus.) Enough, my lord.

DEMETRIUS. (To Theseus.) My lord, fair Helen told me of their travel. I, in fury followed them. Fair Helena in fancy followed me, but my lord, my love is to Hermia. To her, my lord I will for evermore be true.

THESEUS. Fair lovers, you are fortunately met, for in temple by and by with us these couples shall eternally be knit. Away with us to Athens. Three and three, We'll hold a feast in great happiness, come Hippolyta. (All leave.)

Music plays.

Curtain closes and opens to all three couples getting married.

THESEUS. Here come the lovers full of joy and mirth. Joy gentle friends. Accompany your hearts. Come now, what dances shall we have. (He dances with his wife.)
All three couples dance. Wedding celebration.

The End

CPSIA information can be obtained
at www.ICGtesting.com
Printed in the USA
LVOW01s1323260416
485396LV00019B/291/P